SUPERSTARS OF WRESTLING

ROMAN REIGNS

SOUTH HUNTINGTON PUB. LIB.
145 PIDGEGON HILL ROAD
HUNTINGTON STA., NY 11746

BY BENJAMIN PROUDFIT

Gareth Stevens
PUBLISHING

HOT TOPICS

Please visit our website, www.garethstevens.com. For a free color catalog of all our high-quality books, call toll free 1-800-542-2595 or fax 1-877-542-2596.

Cataloging-in-Publication Data

Names: Proudfit, Benjamin.
Title: Roman Reigns / Benjamin Proudfit.
Description: New York : Gareth Stevens Publishing, 2019. | Series: Superstars of wrestling | Includes index.
Identifiers: LCCN ISBN 9781538221099 (pbk.) | ISBN 9781538221075 (library bound) | ISBN 9781538221105 (6 pack)
Subjects: LCSH: Wrestlers--United States--Biography--Juvenile literature. | World Wrestling Entertainment, Inc.--Biography--Juvenile literature.
Classification: LCC GV1196.R454 P67 2019 | DDC 796.812092 B--dc23

First Edition

Published in 2019 by
Gareth Stevens Publishing
111 East 14th Street, Suite 349
New York, NY 10003

Copyright © 2019 Gareth Stevens Publishing

Designer: Sarah Liddell
Editor: Kristen Nelson

Photo credits: Cover, pp. 1, 29 Ron Elkman/Sports Imagery/Contributor/Getty Images Sport/Getty Images; p. 5 Hopeful Duck/Wikimedia Commons; p. 7 Marc Pfitzenreuter/Contributor/Getty Images Sport/Getty Images; p. 9 Mike Zarrilli/Stringer/Getty Images Sport/Getty Images; p. 11 Getty Images/Stringer/Getty Images Sport/Getty Images; pp. 13, 21, 25 FlickrWarrior/Wikimedia Commons; p. 15 Starship.paint/Wikimedia Commons; p. 17 Joachim Sielski/Stringer/Bongarts/Getty Images; p. 19 Shipjustgotreal/Wikimedia Commons; p. 23 Sylvain Lefevre/Contributor/Getty Images Sport/Getty Images; p. 27 CHANDAN KHANNA/Stringer/AFP/Getty Images.

All rights reserved. No part of this book may be reproduced in any form without permission in writing from the publisher, except by a reviewer.

Printed in the United States of America

CPSIA compliance information: Batch #CS18GS: For further information contact Gareth Stevens, New York, New York at 1-800-542-2595.

CONTENTS

The Crowd Goes Wild	4
Family Ties	6
On the Field	8
The Ring Calls	12
What's in a Name?	16
The Shield	18
Seth's Turn	22
Champ Chances	24
Beating the Dead Man	28
The Best of Roman Reigns	30
For More Information	31
Glossary	32
Index	32

THE CROWD GOES WILD

Whether World Wrestling Entertainment (WWE) fans love or hate Roman Reigns, they always make a lot of noise when he enters the ring. Roman was born to be a WWE Superstar—but he still had to work hard to get there!

IN THE RING

Many people in Roman's family were **professional** wrestlers. His father was Sika, a member of the tag team known as the Wild Samoans

FAMILY TIES

Roman was born Leati Joseph Anoa'i on May 25, 1985. His family called him Joe. Roman's dad put a wrestling ring in the backyard of their home in Pensacola, Florida. Roman grew up watching well-known wrestlers practice in it.

IN THE RING

Rikishi, Yokozuna, Rocky Johnson, and even The Rock are all also part of Roman's family. The WWE tag team the Usos are, too!

ON THE FIELD

In high school, Roman was a football star. He went on to start as a defensive tackle for the Georgia Tech Yellow Jackets from 2003 to 2006. Roman did well enough to earn tryouts for teams in the National Football League (NFL).

IN THE RING

One of Roman's high school coaches said of Roman as a football player: "He might not have been the tallest or fastest, but he was the **toughest** by far."

In 2007, Roman tried out for the Minnesota Vikings. He didn't make the team. He was then with the Jacksonville Jaguars for just a few days. In 2008, Roman played in the Canadian Football League (CFL) for the Edmonton Eskimos.

IN THE RING

After one season in the CFL, Roman stopped playing football.

THE RING CALLS

Roman has said that he was already thinking about trying wrestling when he was in the CFL. Once he left football, Roman spent some time working with the Usos for a company run by his sister. After the Usos left for the WWE, Roman had to decide if he wanted to try it, too.

IN THE RING

In 2015, Roman said: "Even as a kid, before I started playing football, I always thought I was going to be a wrestler."

In 2010, WWE signed Roman to wrestle for Florida Championship Wrestling (FCW). Even though Roman came from a family of wrestlers, he'd never wrestled until he started training with WWE. He said that at his tryout, he "blew up" in his first match!

IN THE RING

To "blow up" in a pro wrestling match is to become really tired and not do well because of it.

WHAT'S IN A NAME?

While in FCW, Roman was called Roman Leakee. He and Mike Dalton—later called Tyler Breeze—became the Tag Team Champions! When FCW became WWE NXT in 2012, Roman's in-ring name became Roman Reigns. Soon after, he was brought up to the main WWE **roster**.

TYLER BREEZE

IN THE RING

NXT is the developmental part of WWE. WWE wrestlers may start there to develop, or grow and get better, in the ring.

THE SHIELD

Roman first appeared as part of a group called the Shield. Dean Ambrose and Seth Rollins were the other members. The Shield **debuted** at the Survivor Series **pay-per-view** (PPV) in 2012 and had their first **official** match at TLC a few weeks later.

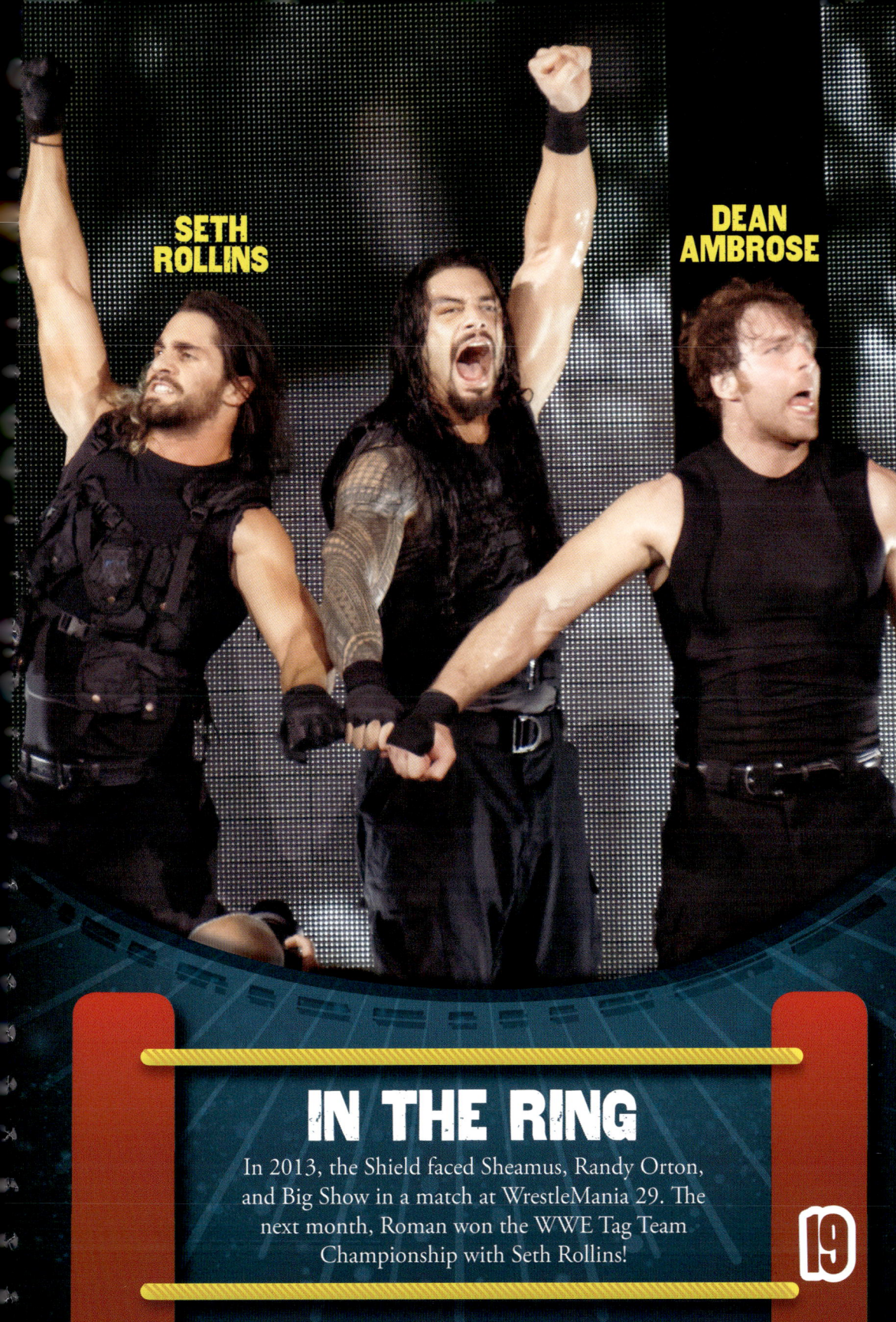

IN THE RING

In 2013, the Shield faced Sheamus, Randy Orton, and Big Show in a match at WrestleMania 29. The next month, Roman won the WWE Tag Team Championship with Seth Rollins!

The Shield was a fan favorite into 2014. Roman began to shine as a singles star, too. He **eliminated** the most Superstars of anyone ever in the Royal Rumble that year. He came in second to Batista in the 30-man match.

IN THE RING

The Shield beat Kane and the New Age Outlaws in a short match at WrestleMania 30 on April 6, 2014.

SETH'S TURN

By June 2014, the Shield had put on great matches against the Wyatt Family and Evolution. At the Payback PPV, the Shield once again beat Evolution. But the next night on *Raw*, Seth Rollins turned on Roman and Dean Ambrose. He joined Evolution!

BRAY WYATT

IN THE RING

Once the Shield broke up, Roman was pushed to the top of the WWE roster. He began fighting for the WWE Heavyweight Championship.

23

CHAMP CHANCES

In January 2015, Roman won the Royal Rumble for a chance at the championship at WrestleMania 31. He faced Brock Lesnar in the main event. But Seth Rollins cashed in his Money in the Bank contract and pinned Roman to win the championship!

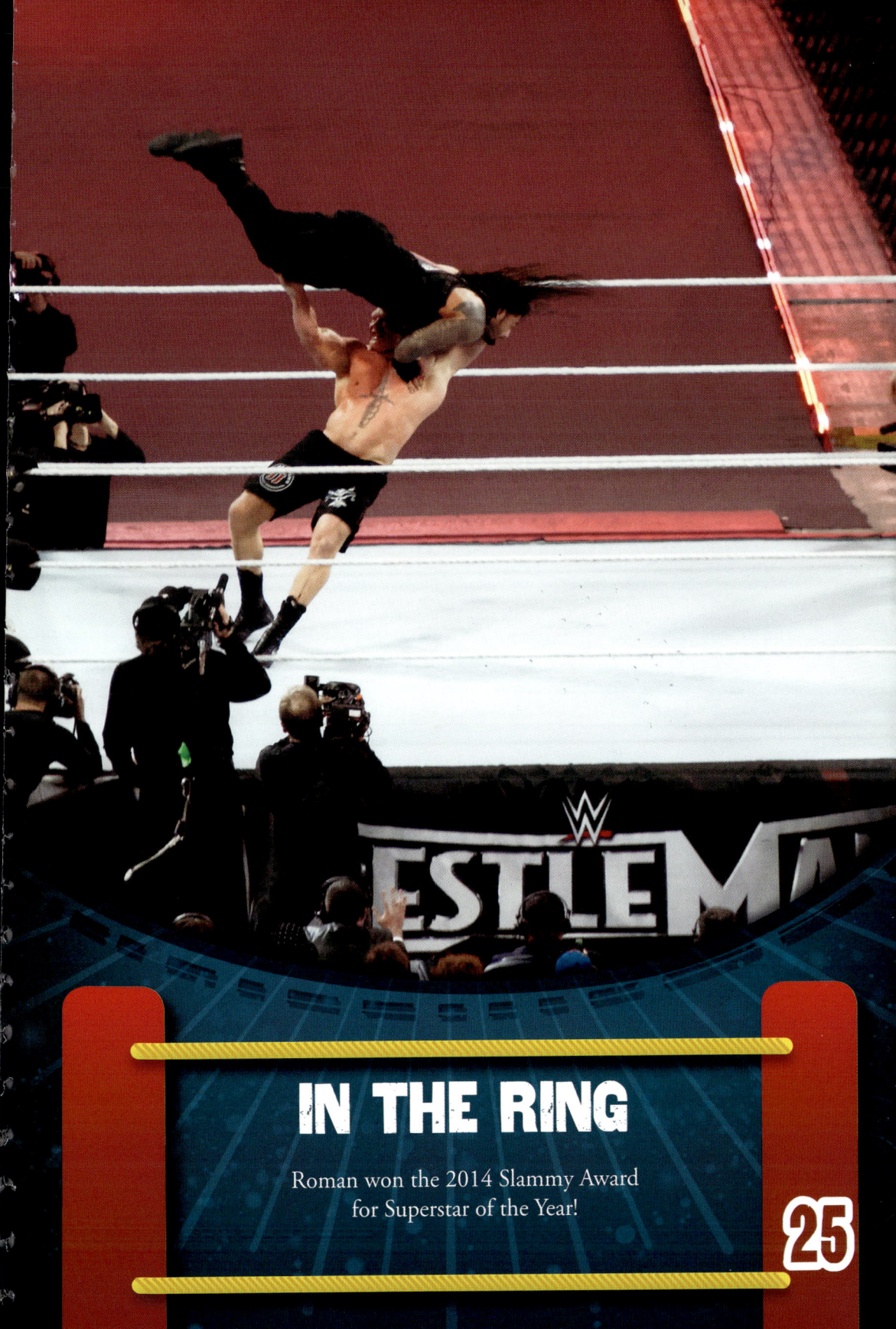

Roman won his first WWE Heavyweight Championship in a match against Dean Ambrose in late 2015. Right then, Sheamus cashed in his Money in the Bank contract, pinned Roman, and took the title! Later, Roman won a rematch with Sheamus and became champion again!

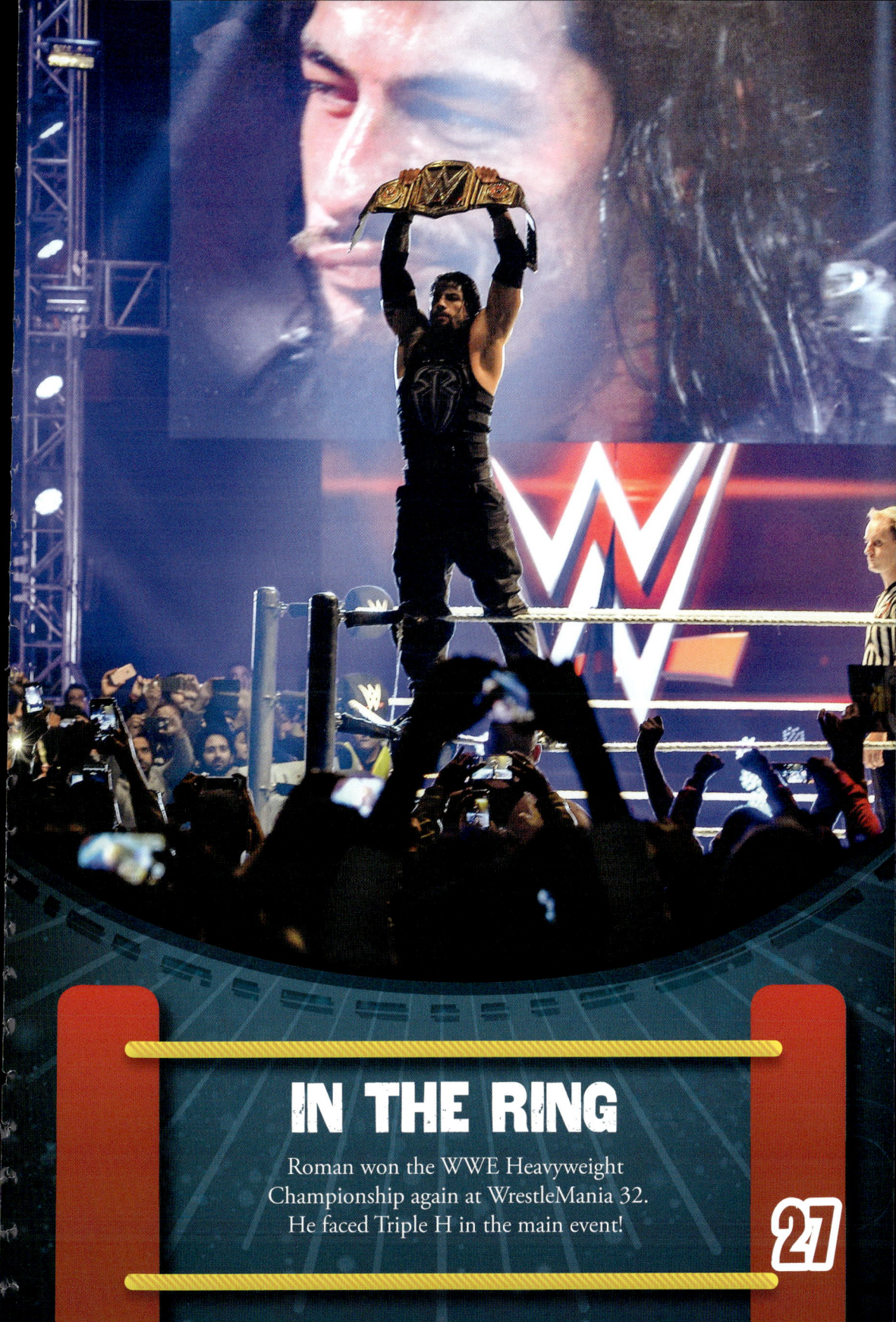

IN THE RING

Roman won the WWE Heavyweight Championship again at WrestleMania 32. He faced Triple H in the main event!

27

BEATING THE DEAD MAN

In April 2017, Roman was again part of the main event of WrestleMania. He faced the Undertaker—and won! This was the biggest match of his life so far. But there's no telling what he'll do next!

IN THE RING

In October 2017, the Shield got back together.

THE BEST OF ROMAN REIGNS

SIGNATURE MOVES
Superman punch, Samoan drop, clotheslines

FINISHING MOVE
spear

ACCOMPLISHMENTS
part of the main event of WrestleMania; WWE World Heavyweight Champion; WWE US Champion; WWE Tag Team Champion; beat the Undertaker

MATCH TO WATCH
TLC 2012 as part of the Shield; Extreme Rules 2016 vs. AJ Styles

FOR MORE INFORMATION

BOOKS

Kortemeier, Todd. *Superstars of WWE*. Mankato, MN: Amicus High Interest, 2017.

Sullivan, Kevin. *WWE Encyclopedia: The Definitive Guide to WWE*. Indianapolis, IN: DK/Prima Games, 2016.

WEBSITES

Roman Reigns
www.wwe.com/superstars/roman-reigns
Find updates about Roman Reigns on his official WWE page.

Roman-Reigns.Net
roman-reigns.net
Check out this fan website for the latest information about Roman's career.

Publisher's note to educators and parents: Our editors have carefully reviewed these websites to ensure that they are suitable for students. Many websites change frequently, however, and we cannot guarantee that a site's future contents will continue to meet our high standards of quality and educational value. Be advised that students should be closely supervised whenever they access the internet.

GLOSSARY

debut: to appear for the first time

eliminate: to get rid of

official: having the support of a group

pay-per-view: an event that can only be seen on a TV channel if viewers pay a fee

professional: earning money from an activity that many people do for fun

roster: the list of people that are on a team

tough: able to do hard work well

INDEX

Ambrose, Dean 18, 19, 22, 26
Evolution 22
football 8, 9, 10, 11, 12, 13
Money in the Bank 24, 26
NXT 16, 17
pay-per-view (PPV) 18, 22
Raw 22
Rollins, Seth 18, 19, 22, 24
Royal Rumble 20, 24
Sheamus 19, 26
Shield, the 18, 19, 20, 22, 23, 28, 30
Superstar 4, 20, 25
Tyler Breeze 16, 17
Undertaker 28, 30
Usos, the 6, 7, 12
World Wrestling Entertainment (WWE) 4, 6, 12, 14, 16, 17, 19, 23, 26, 27, 30
WrestleMania 19, 20, 24, 27, 28, 30
Wyatt Family 22, 23

RECEIVED FEB - 8 2019